## Date Due

|  |  |
|---|---|
|  |  |
|  |  |
|  |  |
|  |  |
|  |  |
|  |  |
|  |  |
|  |  |
|  |  |
|  |  |
|  |  |
|  |  |
|  |  |
|  |  |
|  |  |

The Library of Author Biographies™

# E. L. Konigsburg

The Library of Author Biographies™

# E. L. KONIGSBURG

**Renee Ambrosek**

The Rosen Publishing Group, Inc., New York

Published in 2006 by The Rosen Publishing Group, Inc.
29 East 21st Street, New York, NY 10010

First Edition

**Library of Congress Cataloging-in-Publication Data**

Ambrosek, Renee.
E. L. Konigsburg/Renee Ambrosek.
    p. cm.—(The library of author biographies)
Includes bibliographical references and index.
ISBN 1-4042-0459-8 (lib. bdg.)
ISBN 1-4042-0648-5 (pbk. bdg.)
1. Konigsburg, E. L. 2. Authors, American—20th century—Biography.
3. Children's stories, American—History and criticism. 4. Children's
stories—Authorship. I. Title. II. Series.
PS3561.O459Z53 2006
813'.54—dc22

                                                        2004028906

*Manufactured in the United States of America*

From Contemporary Authors New Revision Series, by Linda Metzger and Deborah A. Straub, 17, Gale Group, © 1986, Gale Group. Reprinted by permission of the Gale Group.

From Contemporary Authors New Revision Series, 39 and 59, Gale Group, © 1992 and 1998, Gale Group. Reprinted by permission of the Gale Group.

From *Something About the Author*, by Anne Commire, 1, Gale Group, © 1973, Gale Group. Reprinted by permission of the Gale Group.

From *Dictionary of Literary Biography: American Writers for Children Since 1960* by Perry Nodelman, 52, Gale Group, © 1986, Gale Group. Reprinted by permission of the Gale Group.

From *E. L. Konigsburg* by Dorrel Thomas Hanks Jr., Twayne Publishers, © 1992, Twayne Publishers. Reprinted by permission of the Gale Group.

*Newbery and Caldecott Medal Books, 1966–1975*, 1975. Reprinted by permission of The Horn Book, Inc., Boston, MA, www.hbook.com.

*The Horn Book Magazine*, September/October 1973 and January/February 1978. Reprinted by permission of The Horn Book, Inc., Boston, MA, www.hbook.com.

Copyright 1986 by the National Council of Teachers of English. Reprinted with permission.

Reprinted with the permission of Atheneum Books for Young Readers, an imprint of Simon & Schuster Children's Publishing Division from *From the Mixed-up Files of Mrs. Basil E. Frankweiler, About the B'nai Bagels*, and *TalkTalk* by E. L. Konigsburg. Text copyright © 1967, 1969, and 1995 E. L. Konigsburg.

# Table of Contents

# Introduction:
# The Scientific Theory
# of E. L. Konigsburg

Elaine Lobl Konigsburg may be one of the most well-rounded authors in the field of children's fiction. Not only has she created fourteen novels for young adults to date, but she has illustrated many of them as well. She has also published three picture books for early readers and a book of essays for adults. Her work includes mysteries, science fiction, historical fiction, short stories, and humorous novels. Konigsburg has indeed left her mark on many genres of literature.

However, this talented author didn't always dream of being a writer. Konigsburg was originally a scientist—she was in her late thirties when she decided to try writing for the first time, following an early retirement from her career in

7

chemistry. Considering the way that Konigsburg has approached her writing career, it seems pretty evident that she wasn't a complete convert from chemistry—she still thinks like a scientist.

There is an old saying that claims that "necessity is the mother of invention." This means that things are invented only after they become a "necessity"— once people realize that something is missing or needed in society, someone will step in just at that moment and invent it. Usually, this saying is used in reference to a scientific or technological break-through, though, not about something artistic like painting or writing.

However, when it comes to an author such as Konigsburg, the saying seems to be very appro-priate—and not just because Konigsburg started out as a scientist. It seems fitting for Konigsburg because she began to write children's books in order to fill a strong need that she saw in society— the need for kids to be able to read books about characters that were a lot like themselves. It shouldn't be surprising, either, that once Konigsburg saw this need, she used the scientific method to help her invent a new type of children's book that would fill the need.

The first step in the scientific method is to iden-tify the problem. Whether Konigsburg realized it at the time, she started this step while she was still a child. Young Elaine grew up in a multicultural community of immigrant families, where money could be tight and life could be difficult. In contrast, all of the characters in the children's books that she read seemed to lead lives that were very different from her own. This bothered young Elaine, and once she grew up, she recognized that it was a "problem"—there were not always books available that spoke to the young readers who hungered for them.

The second step in the scientific method is to develop a hypothesis, or a theory. Konigsburg developed her hypothesis once she had kids of her own. She remembered how much she had wanted to read books about other kids just like herself when she was a child, but there weren't any. She thought about this problem and formed a theory that kids such as her own—kids who were growing up in the suburbs of America—would enjoy and respond to children's books about other kids growing up in suburbs.

Using this theory, she decided to move on to the third step in the scientific method—testing the hypothesis. In order to test the hypothesis, she had to perform an experiment. The best way to test whether kids really did want to read about other kids like themselves is to offer them children's books featuring characters they could relate to, and then see how they respond. Konigsburg's experiment, then, was to write a children's book that featured characters just like her own kids.

The next step in the scientific method is to evaluate the data. This means that at the end of the experiment, you decide whether the results of your experiment prove that your hypothesis is correct. In Konigsburg's case, this evaluation was done for her. In January 1968, Konigsburg discovered that her first two "experiments" had both received awards from the Association for Library Service to Children. Her first experiment, the novel *Jennifer, Hecate, Macbeth, William McKinley, and Me, Elizabeth* (1967), had been placed on the Newbery Honor list, and her second experiment, *From the Mixed-up Files of Mrs. Basil E. Frankweiler* (1967), had won the Newbery Medal.

The Newbery awards are the most important and influential awards in children's publishing. The medal goes to the book that the association considers to be the very best book for children published during the previous year. The Newbery Honor list is for books that were also notable, sort of like the runners-up. Before Konigsburg, no author had ever had two books win Newbery awards during the same year—and no one has done it since.

This unusual feat allowed Konigsburg to "evaluate her data" in a way that she never could have if she had remained unknown. Suddenly everyone in children's publishing knew who E. L. Konigsburg was, and everyone was reading her books. More important, they were recommending her books to the audience that counts—kids. Konigsburg began getting mail from kids all over America, and the mail confirmed that her "scientific experiment" was a success. Her hypothesis was right—kids loved to read about characters just like themselves, and furthermore, they loved to read about them in the pages of Konigsburg's books.

But the scientific method doesn't end there. The last step of the method is to use the results to help identify a new problem. A scientist looks at the questions and problems that came up during the experiment and then uses those questions to help create new experiments. Konigsburg did just that. After reading the fan letters that her new readers were sending to her, she started to realize that her fans were asking her to create new, "different" kinds of characters and situations in her books.

These letters gave her the courage to formulate her next hypothesis, which was that kids want to be challenged when they read. They want to meet new types of people and visit new settings in the books that they read. This hypothesis has served Konigsburg well, since she has spent the rest of her writing career experimenting with characters, settings, and genres. This has led to the amazing diversity that Konigsburg has been able to achieve as an author.

Throughout her career, Konigsburg has approached writing in a very scientific kind of way. Even though she probably wasn't consciously following the scientific method as her career developed, it sure seems like she still thinks like a scientist when she approaches a problem. Certainly in the case of E. L. Konigsburg, necessity has been the mother of invention, time and time again.

# 1 Identifying the Problem

Although Konigsburg was an avid reader growing up, there was nothing about her early childhood that suggested that she would later become a famous children's book writer. She was born Elaine Lobl on February 10, 1930, in New York City, but her family soon moved, trading life in the big city for a series of small, industrialized mill towns in the Northeast.

Young Elaine spent her days in the same ways that most other kids in small Northeastern towns did and still do: going to school, playing with friends, doing her chores. Her family was Jewish and of Hungarian descent. Her father, Adolph Lobl, was a businessman, and her mother, Beulah Klein Lobl, was a homemaker who also helped out in the family shop.

Elaine was the middle child in the family; she has an older sister named Harriett and a younger sister named Sherry. Although she would later describe herself as having been a serious, timid girl, Elaine also remembers a lot of fun times in her childhood:

> I liked to draw, and I loved going to the movies. My favorite movies were the ones starring Ginger Rogers and Fred Astaire, and historical epics like Marie Antoinette. Until I was ten, we lived over my father's store on the main street of town, and we played sidewalk games like Statue, May I?, and Hopscotch, and we could roller-skate when the stores were not busy. Indoors we played Pick-up Sticks, Chinese Checkers (I was good at it), Jacks (never got past twosies), and lots of cards.[1]

Elaine tended to be something of an academic overachiever. She loved any school subject that did not involve music or sports, two areas in which she did not exactly excel. "I was hopeless at both," she says. "All through elementary school our classes were divided into redbirds and bluebirds. The bluebirds were allowed to sing; the redbirds listened. I was a redbird . . . Fortunately, gym and music were never given letter grades."[2]

However, she did love to draw, and art was a passion for her. Her parents encouraged her as an artist, as she explains:

**14**

One day I was supposed to be taking a nap, or something. Instead I went upstairs and drew, copied actually, some comics—I think it was *Li'l Abner* by Al Capp. My mother saw my copies, and she didn't scold me for missing my nap. She praised my drawing. Both of my parents praised me for the drawing—and my father ordered a set of oil paints from the Sears catalog, and got me a little wooden easel, and I painted.[3]

Elaine studied art in school as a young girl, even winning a War Bond art contest when she was in junior high. Unfortunately, by the time Elaine reached high school, she was forced to stop taking art classes, since her high school did not offer art.

Another favorite pastime for young Elaine was reading. Although reading was tolerated in the Lobl household, it wasn't encouraged. Rather, her parents often preferred that Elaine spend her time in more constructive pursuits, such as helping out with the housework. However, reading provided a sneaky escape from doing chores. As she later recalled:

I used to have what my family called dishes diarrhea. Whenever there were dishes to be done, [I] would have to go to the bathroom. The bathroom was the only room in the house with a lock on the door, and I used to go there to read . . . I remember crying so hard as I read the final chapters of *Gone with the Wind* that I kept flushing the toilet so that my parents wouldn't hear me.[4]

# Elementary Inspirations

Elaine's family lived in Phoenixville, Pennsylvania, for the first part of her elementary school career, but relocated to Youngstown, Ohio, when Elaine was in the fifth grade. In Youngstown, Elaine attended William McKinley Elementary School, a place that she later used as a part of her title for her first novel.

It was also at William McKinley that she had an experience that would later serve as the basis for one of her short stories. Halfway through Elaine's sixth-grade year, the Lobls moved outside the school district that included William McKinley Elementary. However, the principal at McKinley arranged for Elaine to finish out the year there, in order to keep her from having to change schools midyear. This meant that Elaine would have to get to school by bus, an uncommon situation in the Youngstown area. Everyone at William McKinley usually walked home for lunch, but Elaine couldn't. She became one of two "bus children" who had to eat lunch at the school. In an interview, Elaine described her experience as a "bus child" at William McKinley:

> I used to go upstairs at lunchtime and draw on the blackboard. Another girl, Roseann Dolores Ansevino, was also being bused to William McKinley—I don't know why. She and I did not get along; in fact, she once called me "a dirty

Jew." However, after I drew a giant fly on the blackboard upstairs, she invited everyone to come and admire it. We got to be friendly.[5]

This story probably sounds very familiar to anyone who has read "Momma at the Pearly Gates," a short story in Konigsburg's book *Altogether, One at a Time*. Konigsburg said in an interview that this is "the only autobiographical account that she has written."[6]

# An Immigrant Community

After Elaine survived being a bus student at William McKinley, the family moved again, this time to Farrell, Pennsylvania. The family stayed in Farrell for a long period of time in comparison to how often they had moved up to that point, and in interviews Konigsburg usually calls Farrell her hometown. Farrell was a small city; at the time, it had a population of 12,500. The city motto was An Industrial City of Friendly People, and like most Northeastern industrial cities, it was a rich mix of many different cultures, as Elaine would later explain:

> Within its population of 12,500, Farrell had the following social clubs: Polish, Bulgarian, Serbian, Romanian, Slovenian, Hungarian, Italian, Carpo-Russ, German as well as Saxon, Greek as well as Macedonian, a Young Men's Hebrew Association,

the Twin City Elks, which was all black, and three Croatian Homes. Members of the club met with a level of social comfort in the alien New World. It was in the privacy of these clubs that the Croats, the Serbs, the Saxons, et cetera, kept alive the traditions and language and memories of the old country while their children were becoming Americans. Each of us children of immigrants was free to keep the customs of our parents or modify them or abandon them. Sometimes we mixed; sometimes we matched. The Zahariou girls and Achilles Mouganis studied Greek after school just as the Jewish kids studied Hebrew after school. The kids whose parents belonged to the Macedonian Club as well as the ones whose parents belonged to the Greek Club all became Americans. As did I.[7]

In short, Elaine's childhood was not very different from the childhood experiences of many youths who grew up during the Great Depression, especially those kids who lived in immigrant communities. America was undergoing a major change in the 1930s, as wave after wave of immigrants came in search of a better life. The United States Census Bureau reports that the number of people who immigrated to America increased from 2.2 million in 1850 (when the first census was done) to 14.2 million by 1930.[8] Most of these immigrants, like Elaine's father, were from central or eastern Europe, and like Elaine's father, many of them settled in communities such as Farrell.

Despite the fact that Elaine's childhood was typical of so many immigrant children, she often felt frustrated when she read the novels for children that were in print at the time—novels that made her feel like her childhood was atypical, or unusual. Elaine spent a lot of time devouring the classic children's novels that the kids of her generation were usually encouraged to read, such as *The Secret Garden* (1911) and *Mary Poppins* (1934). Although in some ways she liked these stories, she also realized that they made her feel uncomfortable about her own childhood. This led to the beginning of Konigsburg's "scientific hypothesis." As she would later say in an interview:

> The books I read as a child . . . were about people who had maids and spoke beautifully polished English. In contrast to this, in our Pennsylvania mill town, people during the Depression were hiring out as maids, and my father lost his business. Some of my school friends spoke with foreign accents because they had learned English from immigrant parents who spoke with foreign accents. As a child I never found any characters in books whose lives resembled those of my classmates, my family and me. [9]

This was a big problem for Konigsburg, especially since she has always had what she describes as a great "faith in words" and in the ability that words have to make things "normal." In other words, Konigsburg understood, even as a child, that when a person reads about a way of life, it makes that way of life seem more normal or "real" to the reader. This presented a dilemma for young Elaine when she read stories about the families in books like *The Secret Garden*. As she said in an interview, "I thought that they were the norm and that the way that I lived was subnormal, waiting for normal."[10] "As I was growing up, I would pick up a book whose jacket would promise that [in it] I would meet typical children in a typical small town," she explains. "Instead, I would meet wimpy lads who took naps and who had faithful servants and patient mothers. I lived in three small towns and never knew anyone [who fit that description]."[11]

Even though young Elaine suspected that her childhood was atypical because it wasn't in any of the books that she read, this was not at all the case. There must have been hundreds of thousands of young readers out there exactly like her. There must have been kids who lived in small American towns or who came from immigrant backgrounds and who longed to see their lives reflected in the plots of the books they read. "It would have been wonderful to read about a Jewish girl living in a small mill town with a father who worked long hours and a mother who 'helped out in the store.' How I would have loved to see my father's rich Hungarian accent translated into print. It would, as I have said, have added a dimension to reality,"[12] Konigsburg says.

This was the beginning of Konigsburg's scientific theory: Children long to see their lives in print; it reaffirms their existence and gives them the reassurance that they need. This would be a theory that Elaine would remember, and remember well, when she had her own children.

# 2 Forming the Hypothesis

While it is true that Farrell, Pennsylvania, might have been a city of limited possibilities for Elaine—there were no art classes nor any mentors to help her develop her artistic, creative side—it is also true that she considered it to have been a peaceful, loving community in which to grow up. It allowed her the opportunity to begin to discover the kind of person she was. As she says:

> Growing up in a small town gives you two things, a sense of your place and a feeling of self-consciousness—self-consciousness about one's education and exposure, both of which tend to be limited. On the other hand, limited possibilities also means creating your own options. A small town allows you to grow in

your own direction, without the bombardment of outside stimulation. You can get a sense of yourself in relation to yourself not to a host of accomplished others.[1]

Perhaps the "limited possibilities" of Farrell impacted Elaine the most when it came time for her to choose a career. Although Elaine was the co-editor of her high school newspaper and she worked on the yearbook, she never considered a career in writing or in the arts. In towns like Farrell, art was not considered to be a profession. Chemistry, on the other hand, was something concrete. It was substantial and real, and people could get jobs in the area of chemistry. Konigsburg explains:

> We had no guidance department in my high school at the time that I went there, and I was the first one in my family to go to college. In the town that I lived in . . . I knew no one who made his living from the arts—I knew no writers, no artists. At that time, a person went away to college to be something; you went away to be an engineer, or you went away to be a chemist. So I went away to be a chemist because I was good at it, and that was the sort of thing that you did.[2]

# College Days

After Elaine graduated as the valedictorian of the Farrell Senior High School class of 1947, she began trying to figure out how she would go about becoming a chemist. The first step would be to figure out how to pay for college—once again, the lack of a high school guidance counselor left Elaine on her own to try to solve her problem. She had never heard of college scholarships, and so she didn't know that they could be a possibility for her.

Finally, Elaine solved the problem on her own, in a very practical way. She devised a plan in which she would alternate each year of schooling with a year working, allowing her to save enough money during each working year to allow her to go back for a college year.

This plan meant that she couldn't go straight to college after high school. Instead, she embarked on her first work year, and she found a job as a book-keeper for the Shenango Valley Provision Company, a meatpacking plant in Sharon, Pennsylvania. Family connections helped her get the job, as one of the co-owners of the plant was Leonard Rosenburg, the husband of her older sister, Harriett. The other co-owner of the plant was a man named Sidney Konigsburg. Sidney had a brother named David, and through her job at the company, Elaine soon had the opportunity to meet David Konigsburg. As she later said, "For me, it was love at first sight."[3]

Elaine and David began dating while she worked at the plant, and they continued the relationship after Elaine started her freshman year at Carnegie Institute of Technology (now called Carnegie Mellon University) in Pittsburgh, Pennsylvania. Although most of her classes were in the science departments, Elaine did have one experience that would influence her later as a writer—her required freshman English writing course. The course was designed for science students, and it focused on teaching her how to write about complicated things in a simple, straightforward manner. "To this day," Konigsburg says, "I cannot think of better training for a writer of children's fiction."[4]

Elaine still intended to leave school at the end of her freshman year in order to spend a second year working until her freshman English professor heard about her plan. Fortunately, he was able to help Elaine get a scholarship and work-study jobs on campus instead. As a result, Elaine was employed variously in the school library, a dormitory laundry, and as a waitress—but the important thing was that she was able to stay continuously enrolled in college. The jobs didn't give her a lot of extra time to develop herself artistically, however, as she remembers:

> College was a crucial "opening up" for me. I worked hard and did well. However, the artistic side of me was essentially dormant. My close college friends never even knew that I could

write and loved to draw. Chemistry majors spend long hours in the lab: some of our courses were full-day labs, and there was not a lot of time for much besides work and schoolwork.[5]

# Life in the Lab

Elaine was able to finish her undergraduate degree in four years, graduating in 1952 with a bachelor of science in chemistry. In July of that same year, she married David Konigsburg, who was then studying for his Ph.D. in industrial psychology at the University of Pittsburgh. Elaine decided to continue her education at the University of Pittsburgh as well, and she was accepted into the school as a master's degree candidate in the department of chemistry.

Konigsburg has said that she entered the master's program "determined to push back the frontier of science," but succeeding only in "pushing back her hairline"[6] after a series of small lab experiment explosions. Twice Elaine blew up the lab sink after she confused the container filled with distilled water with the container filled with flammable acetone. Elaine began to suspect that perhaps a career in chemistry did not match her temperament after all. As she explains:

> I detested the lab work—washing all of those beakers and three-neck, round bottom hand-blown

flasks with ground-glass, custom-fitted stoppers that cost a gazillion dollars each and that had a bad habit of blowing up on me. I hated the smells and having to weigh everything down to the thousandths of a gram—called "milligrams," if I recall. Besides, it's hard to measure what you spill, and I spilled a lot. In a lab you have not only to measure everything—time, temperature, color, amount—you have to keep track of it all in fractions . . . I have never regretted my education in science, and I have never regretted leaving the lab.[7]

# Start with Water

Elaine's break with the lab and her graduate work came after two years at the University of Pittsburgh. In 1954, her husband, David, finished his Ph.D. and got a job in Jacksonville, Florida. Elaine could not have continued her graduate degree at that point even if she had wanted to, since there were no schools in the Jacksonville area that offered a master's degree in chemistry. Instead, Elaine decided to look for a job teaching chemistry. Since she thought that she would not be able to get a job in the Jacksonville public school system without formal teaching certification, she took a position with Bartram School, a private girl's school in the area.

Teaching at Bartram confirmed to Elaine that perhaps science was not actually her major focus of interest after all. "Not only did I always have to ask my students to light my Bunsen burner, having become match-shy, but I became more interested in what was going on inside them [the students] than what was going on inside the test tubes,"[8] she says. Although she began at Bartram with some preconceived notions about private schools and the kind of young person who attended them, she soon began to realize that the young adult experience was more universal than she first believed.

"I had gone to the school with a prejudice against private schools, thinking that they catered to spoiled young women who had it all," she says. "I soon learned that [the girls] were just as uncomfortable inside as I was when I was growing up."[9] Later, when Elaine began to write, she remembered all of the problems and insecurities that the girls at Bartram dealt with—problems and insecurities that were common to most suburban teens.

Her teaching experience taught her another important lesson that she would later use in her writing. As she remembers:

> It was my first time to teach, and I wanted to give it everything I had. I prepared my first class outline and took it to Miss Olga Pratt, the

headmistress. The outline was wonderful—it had philosophy of science, it had history of science, it had everything. Miss Pratt read it through carefully, put it down, paused, looked at me, and said, "Start with water."

She was right, of course. I started with water and the students learned scientific theory and scientific method along the way. The same principle applies to my writing. In all my successful writing, I've been careful to "start with water," with specifics, and in novel writing that means with character and plot. The philosophy must percolate through the story, not vice versa.[10]

# Rekindling the Creative Flame

However, Elaine's new teaching career was soon put on hold while she had her three children. Her eldest, Paul, was born in 1955. Laurie followed in 1956, and Ross completed the trio in 1959. Following Ross's birth, Elaine began to look for something creative to do that would give her a break from the pressures of motherhood and get her outside of the home for a little while. She decided to rekindle her youthful love of painting and drawing.

Elaine began to take painting lessons at the Jacksonville Art Museum in 1959, and she entered a painting in the Jacksonville county fair that same year. The painting won first place. She reentered the contest with another painting again in 1960, and this painting again placed, winning second this time. However, she stopped taking art lessons when she went back to teaching at Bartram School in 1960.

Her second tenure at Bartram School was short-lived, however, as David soon got a new job near New York City. This job forced the family to relocate to Saddle Brook, New Jersey, in 1962. Once there, Elaine started taking art lessons again, this time at the Art Students League in New York City. Every Saturday morning, Elaine would take the train in from her suburban home and attend art class in New York and then spend the afternoons exploring.

After a time, the family relocated once again, this time to Port Chester, New York. While in Port Chester, Elaine's youngest son, Ross, entered kindergarten, and she suddenly found herself with more free time during the day. She used this free time to start writing. As she later described:

> I decided that I would take the mornings—not make a bed, not do the dishes—and write. This turned out to be easier than I expected. We had just moved to Port Chester . . . where I knew no one, so I was spared the endless round of telephone calls from friends, neighbors and acquaintances. I kept the writing secret except from my family.[11]

Now that she was in a position to create stories of her own on paper, Elaine remembered the feeling she had while growing up—her childhood confusion about not seeing any of her own experiences in print. She also began to think about the type of childhood that her own children were now experiencing. As she later told an interviewer:

> When I realized that my kids' growing up was very different from my own but was related to this middle-class kind of child that I had seen when I had taught at the private girls' school, I wanted to write something that reflected their kind of growing up, something that addressed the problems that come about even though you don't have to worry if you wear out your shoes whether your parents can buy you a new pair, something that tackles the basic problems of who am I? What makes me the same as everyone else? What makes me different?[12]

Based on the problem that Elaine identified while she herself was still just a child, she formed a hypothesis: children need to read about themselves in print, and if she wrote about suburban children and the particular types of problems that those children—her children—encounter, they would respond. Konigsburg set out to perform her experiment.

**31**

# 3 Testing the Hypothesis

One of Elaine Konigsburg's essays for adults discusses books that create a "going-home" feeling. In the essay, she defines a "going-home" book as being the kind of book that she longed to read when she was a child, the kind of book that makes the reader say, "That book, that chapter, that character sure struck home."[1]

However, looking back, she realizes, "Now I thank goodness that there were no going-home books for me when I was a child. Because I worried that my own three children would miss them as they started growing up, and I began to write so that they would have a book that was on target for them, a book that would reflect their kind of growing up as books had not reflected mine."[2]

# True Life Observations

In fact, Konigsburg's first novel would reflect how her kids were growing up in a pretty specific way— it was based on one of their real experiences. Following the move to Port Chester, Konigsburg's daughter, Laurie, was having trouble finding new friends. As Konigsburg remembers:

> Laurie was somewhat independent, somewhat shy, and did not mix readily with other children. At first she walked to school with her brother, but when he found friends and boy interests, this ceased and Laurie walked alone and played alone. The girls in her class, most of whom had lived in the neighborhood for some time, had their friends and did not go out of their way or interrupt their established routines to welcome a newcomer. It was only after a number of weeks had passed that Laurie came running into the house, asking to go play at the home of a friend. With enormous relief, I asked the friend's name and address and gave permission. Then I looked out the window to see a tall, proud, Negro girl striding off down the street, with Laurie following with obvious respect. Two outsiders had found each other, and a friendship had begun.[3]

Laurie's experience of being an outsider was quickly molded into the plot line of Konigsburg's first novel, *Jennifer, Hecate, Macbeth, William McKinley, and Me, Elizabeth*. In the novel, Elizabeth, the narrator, has recently moved to town and is having trouble making friends at her new school. One day while walking to school, she meets Jennifer, another outsider. Jennifer confides in Elizabeth that she is a witch, and Jennifer carries herself with such confidence and dignity that Elizabeth begins to believe her. Jennifer agrees to take Elizabeth on as an apprentice witch, and their friendship grows around this shared, secret apprenticeship.

However, the friendship is tested when it comes time to use their pet toad as an ingredient in their witches' brew. Just as Jennifer is poised to add the toad into the cauldron, Elizabeth stops her and saves the animal's life. Without the pretense of the witch's apprenticeship, Jennifer and Elizabeth's friendship abruptly comes to a halt. After Elizabeth spends the next few days reflecting on the friendship, she begins to realize that Jennifer wasn't a witch after all. Just as Elizabeth finishes figuring out how Jennifer had fooled her, Jennifer arrives at Elizabeth's house to make up with her. At the end of the novel, the two have reestablished their friendship, this time based not on the fantasy of witchcraft, but on genuine affection for one another.

# The Elements of Konigsburg

When Konigsburg wrote *Jennifer*, she had to decide how to address the fact that the character of Jennifer (like Laurie's new friend) was black. In her first draft of the novel, Konigsburg didn't mention Jennifer's ethnicity at all, instead simply showing the fact off in the pictures, illustrating Jennifer as being black.

However, when the book was getting ready to be published, Konigsburg's editor asked her, "Why . . . if Jennifer is a Negro, does the text not say so. Elizabeth is forthright enough to be casual about it, I would think."[4] Konigsburg considered this and agreed, slipping the reference to Jennifer's race nonchalantly into the middle of the book.

This detail gave *Jennifer* an element that was unusual for children's books at the time—an inter-racial friendship in which the "interracial" aspect was not the central issue of the book. This is the beginning of a trend that Konigsburg would repeat again and again in her books. Her plots focus more on relationships and the honest experiences of young adults rather than rely on gimmicks or hot-button issues.

*Jennifer* also contains another element that Konigsburg relies on again and again in her novels:

humor. Konigsburg recognizes that kids, especially smart kids, very often communicate through humor, and both Elizabeth and Jennifer are very funny (although each in a different way), which makes them seem more realistic and honest.

Konigsburg had no choice but to get it right and portray kids honestly, even though this was only her first attempt at writing a kid's novel. She was writing for some very tough critics—her own kids. Every morning she sat down to work on her book, and every afternoon, when her kids came home for lunch, she would read to them what she had written that morning while they had been gone. This is how Konigsburg could keep her writing authentic; she knew that if her kids laughed at what she had written, they approved of it. "They laugh or they don't," she says. "Which means that I revise or I don't."[5]

# Exhibit A

By the end of 1966, Konigsburg had finished with *Jennifer, Hecate, Macbeth, William McKinley, and Me, Elizabeth* and sent it in to the Atheneum Publishing Company for consideration. She asked that the book be published under the name E. L. Konigsburg instead of Elaine Konigsburg because she thought that it sounded more mysterious and professional, and it also reminded her of E. B. White, one of her own favorite authors. Jean Karl, the woman who would be Konigsburg's editor for almost every book of her career thus far, received the manuscript of *Jennifer*. She later wrote about how the book came to be printed:

> [The book] arrived at Atheneum unheralded. It simply came in one day with the afternoon mail. The letter with it said, "Enclosed is a manuscript . . . which I would like you to consider for publication. I have also enclosed several sample illustrations, which I hope you will like. Thank you. Sincerely, Elaine L. Konigsburg."
>
> I'd like to be able to report that the manuscript was read and accepted within a few days. But such is not the way with unannounced material, or almost any material, for that matter . . . So it was several months before Elaine Konigsburg climbed the four flights of stairs to the children's department . . . to discuss her book.
>
> She was relatively short, had dark hair, and dark eyes that glinted with an awareness of the foolishness and fun in the world. Her conversation was as pungent and as full of rich humor as her book. But there was a dignity and a sense of solidity about her that gave her wit and humor, depth and dimension, and made it apparent that this was not a one-book author.[6]

**37**

# Exhibit B

Before Jean Karl even agreed to publish *Jennifer*, Konigsburg had already started work on her second novel, *From the Mixed-up Files of Mrs. Basil E. Frankweiler*. Once again, she drew on her observations of her own children for the basis of her story. She had been reading a book that told an old story of some proper and dignified English children who had been kidnapped by pirates, and as a result they threw aside their proper English upbringing and grew up to be wild pirates themselves.

Konigsburg had just recently read this story when her family went on a vacation to Yellowstone National Park. The family decided to have a picnic, but they couldn't find a picnic table in the park. At Elaine's suggestion, they decided to have their feast of salami sandwiches, potato chips, chocolate milk, and cupcakes in a clearing. However, almost immediately upon setting up the picnic, the Konigsburg children began to complain about every aspect: the chocolate milk was warm, the cupcake frosting was melting, and there were ants. Writing about the picnic later, Konigsburg said:

> I thought to myself that if my children ever left home, they would never become barbarians, even if they were captured by pirates. Civilization was not a veneer to them; it was a crust. They would

want at least all of the comforts of home, plus a few dashes of extra elegance. Where, I wondered, would they ever consider running to if they ever left home? They certainly would never consider any place less elegant than the Metropolitan Museum of Art.[7]

And that is precisely where Claudia and Jamie Kincaid, the two main characters in *From the Mixed-up Files of Mrs. Basil E. Frankweiler*, go when they run away from home. In *Files*, Claudia, the eldest child in her family, has decided to leave home in search of adventure. She has planned her escape carefully—she knows exactly where she is going and exactly how to get there, right down to the train schedule that will take her from her suburb into New York City.

To help with the financial aspect of the plan, Claudia recruits her second-youngest brother, Jamie. Jamie is good with money and has already amassed a small fortune that he agrees to contribute toward the plan—more than $24. Claudia and Jamie arrive in New York and successfully begin living in the Metropolitan Museum of Art, escaping the notice of the guards and bathing in the museum fountain at night.

After a few days of this adventure, Claudia and Jamie encounter the museum's newest acquisition, a statue of a marble angel that may or may not have been sculpted by Michelangelo. Determined to solve the mystery of who carved the statue, the two kids set out to find Mrs. Frankweiler, the rich widow who sold the statue to the museum. Mrs. Frankweiler tells them that the secret to the statue's origin can be found in her filing cabinets, and if the children want to know the secret, they must find the file themselves. After a considerable amount of deduction, the kids find the file and learn the secret. Armed with this new secret to keep between them, they finally feel ready to go back home again.

Many readers have questioned whether there was ever a real statue like the angel in *Files*, and in fact, there was. Konigsburg based the story on another statue called *The Lady with the Primroses*, which the Met had purchased for $225. The sculptor was unknown, but the museum suspected that the statue might have been carved by a famous sculptor from the Italian Renaissance. To this day, however, the identity of the sculptor is a mystery.

*Files* was another success for Konigsburg. Once again, Konigsburg's characters depict very realistic and honest portrayals of middle-class kids, and once again, they are very funny (with most of the best lines going to smart-alecky Jamie), as seen in the passage where Claudia first explains the plan to Jamie:

"Here's the plan. Listen carefully."

Jamie squinted his eyes and said, "Make it complicated, Claude. I like complications."

Claudia laughed. "It's got to be simple to work. We'll go on Wednesday because Wednesday is music lesson day. I'm taking my violin out of its case and am packing it full of clothes. You do the same with your trumpet case. Take as much clean underwear as possible and socks and at least one other shirt with you."

"All in a trumpet case? I should have taken up the bass fiddle."[8]

When Konigsburg finished *Files*, she sent it to her editor, Jean Karl. Karl wrote about receiving this manuscript as well:

*From the Mixed-up Files of Mrs. Basil E. Frankweiler* arrived in the afternoon mail on July 1, 1966. It was not unheralded. The accompanying letter read: "Suburban children are still very much on my mind; I submit Exhibit B: my manuscript . . . I am enclosing only one sample drawing— one of the bed in which the children slept. I hope you will like Claudia and Jamie Kincaid and Mrs. Frankweiler, too. Sincerely, Elaine L. Konigsburg." It was read almost immediately and with such delight that it seemed imperative to publish it as soon as possible. It was too good to keep from children (and adults) for any longer than absolutely necessary. It was scheduled for fall of 1967.[9]

With that, Konigsburg had unwittingly performed her experiment. She felt that kids would respond to books that featured characters like themselves, and she delivered with two books that fit that description. With Jennifer, Elizabeth, Claudia, and Jamie, Konigsburg had succeeded in giving young readers some of the most funny, believable, middle-class, and suburban characters that had ever been created in children's literature up to that point in time. Even more important, the characters were realistic. They had to be; they were created from the observations Konigsburg had made while watching her own kids. Now the experiment was complete, and it was time to assess the results—and the results were stunning.

# 4 Evaluating the Data

The Konigsburgs were packing when the call came. David Konigsburg had recently accepted a position that relocated the family back down to Jacksonville again, and they were getting ready to move from their temporary apartment in Jacksonville to their new home. The call came early in the morning, informing Elaine Konigsburg that her first two novels had achieved an unprecedented honor; *Files* had won the Newbery Medal and *Jennifer* had won a Newbery Honor Book listing. Konigsburg was stunned by the news. "Did you know that joy can move book cartons? And dishes and even major appliances—if not mountains? I have never known such unmitigated, out-loud joy,"[1] she later wrote to her editor.

Obviously, Konigsburg's experiment had been successful. The Newbery awards focused attention on her two books, and the attention ensured that the books got into the hands of an excited and appreciative audience. Letters began pouring in from young readers across the country, telling Konigsburg how much they loved the books. Konigsburg's hypothesis was accurate—kids were enjoying reading about other kids. More specifically, they enjoyed reading about suburban, smart, normal, funny, middle-class kids—kids with the same insecurities and problems that they were dealing with themselves.

It was time to start book number three. Once again, the experiences of her own children provided the inspiration for her work. Her son Paul was by this time becoming more involved with sports, and Konigsburg took an active interest in his games. Not content to be an uninformed spectator, Konigsburg began to school herself in the finer aspects of baseball. Her husband later explained:

> Not satisfied with superficial knowledge, Elaine studied the official rule books. Serious discussions were held at the dinner table about the merits of a drag bunt and when it was wiser to run and hit instead of hit and run. We even got her to Shea and Yankee Stadiums where she let her opinions about the managers' decisions be known.[2]

That new knowledge of baseball found its way into her next book, *About the B'nai Bagels* (1967). Narrated by twelve-year-old Mark Setzer, *Bagels* tells the story of Mark and his involvement with the B'nai B'rith neighborhood Little League team, nicknamed the B'nai Bagels. Mark, like many twelve-year-olds, is beginning to experience a lot of changes in his life, and *Bagels* is an explanation of how he deals with the curveballs that life throws him, both on and off the field.

His loving but somewhat overbearing Jewish mother has been selected as his team's new manager, and she selects Mark's older brother as the team's new coach. Although Mark hopes that this will raise his profile on the team, he soon realizes that they both are so serious about making sure that they don't show favoritism that he almost begins to feel a little overlooked.

Adding to the list of things complicating Mark's life is the loss of his best friend, Hersch, who has recently moved across town to a different school district. Mark also has to contend with preparing for his upcoming bar mitzvah, with his crush on his friend's sister, and with the racism of one of his teammates. Throw in a major scandal about cheating during the Little League tournament, and you begin to understand the weight of the problems that Mark deals with during the course of the book.

Once again, Konigsburg creates characters that are very realistic and places them in situations and settings that are immediately recognizable to the reader. Mark is a normal, smart, and occasionally confused and put-upon Little League team member growing up in the suburbs, dealing with all of the problems that a life in the suburbs entails for a twelve-year-old.

And once again, humor plays a huge role in telling the story. Although Mark himself has a wry sense of humor, most of the major laughs go to his mother, Mrs. Setzer, a character who complains, begs, exaggerates, and admonishes, but who ultimately shows herself to be very loving and wise. Mrs. Setzer has a habit of staring at the ceiling as if addressing God himself, praying aloud about her worries and her demands. As Mark describes her, "Mom was holding a slotted spoon and addressing God. Up until the time I began Sunday School, I thought that He lived in the light fixture on our kitchen ceiling."[3]

## A Recurring Theme and Target

Along with her realism and use of humor, however, it becomes obvious with *Bagels* that Konigsburg also repeats a theme with all of her books. This theme is identity. All of Konigsburg's books deal with characters who are trying to figure out who they are in the world and where they fit in.

At first, however, Konigsburg wasn't consciously addressing this theme. She didn't even notice that she was repeating it until she read a critic's review pointing it out. Upon reflection, she agreed that she was creating all of her books around this basic problem. She comments:

> I didn't know until I had read it in that article, that, yes, that was what I had been writing about. I've written some novels since that, and even though I'm not aware of the fact, after I look it over I see that I've written about identity again . . . I think that each author really has a theme and Identity apparently is mine . . . My concerns are still the same, and I happen to think they're probably the most basic concerns that middle-age children have: Who am I? What makes me the same as everyone else? What makes me different from everyone else? If a child has solved the problem of his creature comforts, I don't think there are any more severe problems that face the middle-age child.[4]

Middle-age children are generally between the ages of eight and twelve and consistently seem to be Konigsburg's target audience. When asked why she keeps aiming all of her novels at this audience, Konigsburg points back to her recurring theme of identity as an answer, saying,

> It is at that age that the serious question of child-hood is asking for an answer. Kids want acceptance from their peers, but in two different, opposing ways: They want to be like everyone else and they want to be different from everyone else. So the question is: How do you reconcile these opposing longings?[5]

Konigsburg's daughter, Laurie, explains her theme of identity further in the essay she wrote after her mom won her second Newbery Medal:

> Mom always lets her characters speak for them-selves. At the same time, she persists in having them speak to the core of her readers. Thirty years has not changed the fundamental identity of Mom's audience—middle-age children who crave acceptance by their peers as desperately as they yearn to be appreciated for their differences. E. L. Konigsburg's success can be attributed to the fact that when children read any of her novels, they see themselves, and they laugh.[6]

# Success!

It would seem that there is a large population of middle-age readers in the world who like to see themselves in the novels of E. L. Konigsburg. Since its publication in 1967, *Files* has managed to sell more than 3 million copies in paperback and is the forty-first best-selling children's paperback book of all time, according to figures given by *Publishers Weekly*.[7] Konigsburg says that she appreciates every one of her fans, explaining that she thinks that there are usually three different types of readers.

The first type of reader consists of kids who simply have a talent and love for reading and who seem to enjoy it from a very early age. The second group is made up of kids who are good at reading but don't really have a natural love for it. The last group consists of kids who think of reading as a chore and don't do it unless they are forced. Konigsburg says of these three groups:

> I can tell you that there is no greater compliment than having your work cherished by one of the first kind of reader, someone who has read a lot and chooses your book out of a vast experience of reading. There is also no greater compliment than hearing from a young man in Pennsylvania, "I never liked reading until I read you." And in that middle category—those kids that are skilled but do not take great pleasure in reading— imagine, the joy of being chosen by someone who otherwise reads only assignments. So I guess you could say that I love all of my readers,

for I do. I think that they are wonderful, and I like it when they think that I am. Don't we all want to be wonderful to someone?[8]

Considering the sales figures from *Files* alone, it appears that there is a large population of readers who consider Konigsburg to be wonderful. She filled a gap in children's literature from the very beginning of her career, realizing that kids needed to see themselves in print. She responded to this need by writing a series of novels that dealt with one of the most common problems of suburban, middle-class children, the difficulty of carving out an identity. Even better, she wrote about this theme in a very realistic but funny way. Konigsburg proved that kids would respond to books about characters like themselves, characters who shared their experiences. Her scientific method approach to writing was a success.

It was now time for the final step: reevaluation. Konigsburg took the data from her experiment—the letters that she was getting from her new fans—and used that data to modify her experiment. As she told the Educational Paperback Association,

After I won the Newbery Medal, children all over the world let me know that they liked books that take them to unusual places where they meet unusual people . . . readers let me know that they like books that have more to them than meets the eye.[9]

Konigsburg, a true scientist at heart, knew that this data suggested that she should now branch out some and modify her experiment to reflect the new things she had learned about her audience.

# 5 Modifying the Experiment

If Konigsburg's fans were truly interested in books that introduced them to unusual people, they were to be rewarded with her fourth novel, *(George)*, published in 1970. In this work, Konigsburg creates George, one of her most unusual characters to date. The novel tells the story of Ben Carr, a gifted science student with a secret. Ben has a "concentric twin" named George. George speaks to Ben subconsciously (and on rare occasion aloud), helps to guide him in social situations, and provides him with assistance on a variety of mental tasks, such as memorization.

When Ben's stepmother finds out about George, she concludes that Ben is mentally ill.

The family steps in to get Ben psychiatric help, but by this time George has fallen silent on his own, angered over Ben's overzealous need to be accepted by one of his older classmates. George returns just in time to save Ben after he uncovers the illegal activity of his older classmate, an activity that threatens the funding of the science department at Ben's school.

At first glance, this odd plot seems substantially different from those of Konigsburg's earlier books. However, the main elements still apply in this work—(George) deals with suburban characters, and there is still ample use of humor. And the book deals specifically with Konigsburg's main theme, identity.

Although many readers have assumed that Ben is a schizophrenic or mentally ill character, Konigsburg has consistently denied this in interviews, preferring to think of the work as simply a more literal examination of her recurring theme of identity. She pointed out in a *Contemporary Authors* interview, "I don't really think that Ben is a schizophrenic. It's a very strong feeling I have that when you're a youngster, you're much more in touch with your inner self. The peer pressure begins about sixth grade—sometimes now about fifth grade—to pull you toward what is socially acceptable to that group. You have to stay in touch with this inner self."[1] Although many critics were not enthusiastic about *(George)*, a few agreed with David Rees when he claimed, "*(George)* is probably Elaine Konigsburg's finest achievement so far . . . a light-hearted, genuinely comic novel."[2]

## *Altogether*

Konigsburg's next effort would also be different, but this time the difference would be in genre. In 1971, Konigsburg published *Altogether, One at a Time*, her first book of short stories. Four stories are included in *Altogether*. The first, "Inviting Jason," revolves around a young man who does not want to invite a learning-disabled classmate to his sleepover. "The Night of the Leonids" tells the story of a young man and his grandmother as they attempt to watch a meteor shower that only occurs every thirty-three years. Konigsburg tackles her first supernatural tale in "Camp Fat," a story about a girl who gets sent to "fat camp" and encounters a particularly odd counselor there. Finishing the collection is the story that Konigsburg has referred to as being the only "autobiographically based" work she's ever written, "Momma at the Pearly Gates."

The critical reviews for this book were generally positive. Konigsburg also seems to realize that these stories are something special. When an interviewer asked her what piece of her own writing came closest to the ideal that she'd had in mind, Konigsburg answered, "I think that as far as my writing goes, the short stories come the closest, but it's much easier to write an excellently crafted short story because it's shorter and there's less room for error—if you want to call it error."[3]

## New Experiments

Konigsburg returned to novels with her next work, but this time she surprised her readers by departing from her usual suburban setting. *A Proud Taste for Scarlet and Miniver* (1973) is Konigsburg's first historical novel. It tells the story of Eleanor of Aquitaine, a queen of France and England during the Middle Ages. Eleanor's biography is told through the narrative of four different characters, all of whom are in heaven awaiting the arrival of Eleanor's husband, King Henry, who has been detained in purgatory.

The critics were firmly divided about this book— it seems to be a book that readers either love or hate. Some of the critics agreed with Alice Miller Bregman, who said in a *School Library Journal* review, "Konigsburg fans will be disappointed in [this book, which is an] out-of-sync approach to history as fiction . . . Middle graders, without a better foundation in 12th-Century history than most American curriculums offer, will be confused by the catalog of events."[4]

However, some sided more with critics such as Paul Heins, who wrote in the *Horn Book Magazine* that Konigsburg had "succeeded in making history amusing as well as interesting."[5] Either way, with *A Proud Taste for Scarlet and Miniver*, Konigsburg had unquestionably fulfilled her readers' requests for stories about unusual people in unusual places.

Konigsburg returned to more familiar territory once more with her next book, *The Dragon in the Ghetto Caper*. This 1974 novel tells the story of Andy Chronister, a suburbanite young man with a fascination for dragons and detective stories. Andy is befriended by Edie Yakots, an adult who shares Andy's interest in dragons. The two characters become enmeshed in an accidental detective story of their own after they are implicated in an illegal numbers-running scheme, or form of lottery. Although in this novel Konigsburg returned to an element (funny suburbia) that had earlier been very popular with her readers, *Dragon* failed to make much of an impression on readers or critics, possibly because they had started to expect something newer or more innovative from Konigsburg following *A Proud Taste*.

However, Konigsburg's next novel, *The Second Mrs. Giaconda* (1975), is definitely more innovative. In her second historical novel, Konigsburg offers a solution to the mystery of why Leonardo da Vinci chose to paint Mona Lisa, a rather plain and unknown merchant's wife, instead of taking commissions from Italy's most powerful and beautiful citizens.

Even in this foreign setting, however, Konigsburg continues to deal with her common theme of identity, suggesting that da Vinci's personality is only made complete with the presence of Salai, his irresponsible, unpredictable apprentice. It is Salai who convinces da Vinci that he must paint the second Mrs. Giaconda, Mona Lisa. Once again, the reviews for this novel are mixed, with many of the critics repeating the same criticisms that were made of *A Proud Taste of Scarlet and Miniver*.

In 1976, Konigsburg experimented once more—this time to a better response. *Father's Arcane Daughter* tells the story (in flashback) of siblings Winston and Heidi Carmichael and the young woman who shows up at their home one day, claiming to be Caroline Carmichael, the sister who had been kidnapped from the Carmichael family long before Winston and Heidi were born. This novel was Konigsburg's first mystery, and it is also her first book to be told through flashbacks. Perry Nodelman echoed many critics when he wrote, "This novel may be Konigsburg's most daring experiment . . . Konigsburg has found a way of communicating her rich perception of the subtleties in human relationships in a book that is surprisingly easy to read and to understand."[6]

## A Return to Funny Suburbia

Following *Father's Arcane Daughter*, Konigsburg returned again to what she has become best known for: works with a contemporary, humorous suburban setting. First, she offered her readers another collection of short stories with 1979's *Throwing Shadows*. She followed this in 1982, with *Journey to an 800 Number*, the funny tale of preppy Maximilian "Bo" Stubbs and his summer with his father, an aging hippie who wrangles a "traveling show camel" for a living. In 1986, Konigsburg published *Up from Jericho Tel*, the first supernatural tale that she had offered her readers since the short story "Camp Fat" in *Altogether, One at a Time*. However, despite the differences in genre, all three of these books are once again united by the common hallmarks of Konigsburg's work—they are witty tales of suburban children developing and dealing with the issues of their own identities.

In 1991, Konigsburg took a temporary vacation from novels for the middle-age child and instead tried her hand at drawing picture books for younger readers. Just as she used her own children for the models of the sketches of the characters in her early works, she turned to her grandchildren to provide her with the inspiration for characters in her young reader picture books, *Samuel Todd's Book of Great Colors* (1990), *Samuel Todd's Book of Great Inventions* (1991), and *Amy Elizabeth Explores Bloomingdale's* (1992).

Konigsburg returned to the funny, suburban children's novel in 1993, with the book *T-Backs, T-Shirts, COAT and Suit*. This novel explores the issues of censorship, religious fundamentalism, and (of course) identity, as the central character, twelve-year-old Chloe, tries to live through a summer at her Aunt Bernadette's house in Florida.

## New Innovations

Departing from her usual audience, in 1995 Konigsburg published a book aimed at adults. The result, *TalkTalk: A Children's Book Author Speaks to Grown-Ups*, consists of a series of essays that Konigsburg had written over the past three decades.

However, in 1996, Konigsburg returned to her preteen audience once more with the stunning novel *The View from Saturday*. The book revolves around Noah, Nadia, Ethan, and Julian, a group of outsiders who come together to form an unlikely but solid friendship while they bond as members of a school quiz bowl team. Each one of the four central characters in the novel takes a turn at narrating the events, allowing the reader to get a complete perspective on the action in the book and giving a unique opportunity to see how the four pieces of the friendship fit together.

*The View from Saturday* received rave reviews from readers and critics alike, and went on to win the 1997 Newbery Medal, marking the second time that Konigsburg had received that honor. In her *School Library Journal* review of the book, Julie Cummins concluded, "Brilliant writing melds with crystalline characterizations in this sparkling story that is a jewel in the author's crown of out-standing work."[7]

In an essay about the second Newbery Medal, Konigsburg's daughter, Laurie, noticed, "Although the inspiration for these Newbery books was as disparate as the three decades that separate their publication, their theme is the same. In fact, every one of E. L. Konigsburg's fourteen novels are about children who seek, find, and ultimately enjoy who they are."[8]

The characters in Konigsburg's next novel don't immediately seem to be enjoying who they are, however. *Silent to the Bone* (2000), a smart, edgy mystery story, is the darkest work of Konigsburg's career. It begins with the 911 call that Branwell Zamborska places in order to get help for his infant half sister, who has become unconscious. However, Branwell doesn't speak during the 911 call; in fact, it seems that the trauma of the accident has rendered Branwell permanently mute. Accused of causing the accident, Branwell is taken to a juvenile detention facility, where he receives visits from his best friend, Connor. With the help of his half sister Margaret, Connor becomes determined to solve the mystery of what made Branwell stop speaking.

Konigsburg revisits Connor's family again in her last novel to date, *The Outcasts of 19 Schuyler Place*. However, this time the novel centers on Margaret Rose Kane, Connor's older half sister in *Silent to the Bone*. In *Outcasts*, the narrator takes us back in time to the events of Margaret's twelfth summer. After an unpleasant stint in summer camp, Margaret is rescued by her two beloved Hungarian uncles. However, her satisfaction from having escaped from camp quickly dissolves when she discovers that the huge works of art that her uncles have devoted their lives to constructing are about to be demolished. Once again, Konigsburg returns to the elements that are so often in her work—humor, middle-class kids, and a search for identity. In *Outcasts*, Konigsburg blends these elements within the character of Margaret, one of the most striking characters she has yet created, and the combination produces a very strong novel.

Konigsburg has said in interviews that she is once again working on another novel, but she's "superstitious about talking about a work in progress,"[9] so her readers will have to wait to see what she has in store next. It's safe to bet, though, that she will most likely be continuing to modify her experiment and present her readers with another type of story that she thinks they will respond well to.

# 6 A Peek Inside the Process

Anyone who has ever performed an experiment for science class or a science fair project knows that there is a lot of work that goes into creating a good experiment. To begin with, a good scientist has to be creative in order to think up a project. The scientist also has to do all of the background research that the project requires. Finally, the scientist has to have the discipline needed to finish the whole experiment, even if it takes a long time to complete. Considering Elaine Konigsburg's background in science, it probably isn't surprising that the same things are true of her writing process.

Konigsburg says that all of her ideas for her books come from her personal experiences in some way, but it is her creativity that allows her to take everyday events and mold them into an interesting plot. As she said in an interview:

> I get my ideas from things I've read, people I've met, situations I know about. The important thing about ideas is the coming together of character, place, theme and plot. I'm going to suggest something. Suppose you take an ordinary event, and ask yourself, "what if?" Suppose you get on the school bus tomorrow morning. What if suddenly the school bus driver can only speak Hungarian and your best friend won't speak to you at all? Suppose you get up in the morning to see the sunrise, and what if the trees in the light of day are all blue instead of green and the sky is red instead of blue? Suppose that you're sitting in school, and what if you are suddenly not right-handed but left-handed? What if you are suddenly blue-eyed instead of brown-eyed? Take an ordinary event and ask yourself "what if?" When it all comes together, that's what getting an idea really is.[1]

## Research

Once Konigsburg uses her creativity to come up with a new idea, she has to do the hard work of research. Konigsburg says that she spends a lot of time doing research for her books. It seems pretty obvious that she would have to do a lot of research when she writes one of her historical novels since she has to get all of the background of the characters and the time period just right. What might not be so obvious, though, is the amount of research that even her contemporary books require. For example, in one interview she explained the research that she had to do for *Journey to an 800 Number*, a book that featured a pet camel:

> I knew very little about camels. I called the zoo and they knew very little about camels. It happens that my daughter was doing a project at Cornell University where they have an enormous agriculture school, so she looked up a lot about camels for me, which are remarkable animals by the way. Even though it wasn't necessary to have a lot of information about camels in the book, I didn't feel I could write about a camel unless I knew about them.[2]

Konigsburg even did extensive research for her most well-known book, *From the Mixed-up Files of Mrs. Basil E. Frankweiler*, as her editor Jean Karl wrote:

> Mrs. Konigsburg spent most of her free time in fall 1966 posing her own children at appropriate spots in the museum, under the eyes of the suspicious guards, and carefully observing the routines. The results produced a book that comes

as close to possibility and accuracy as the museum's understandable bent toward secrecy will allow. In fact, the book even includes the museum's own map made from the original art prepared for a visitor's guide to the museum, and used with the museum's permission.[3]

# "Finish!"

Once all of the research is done, Konigsburg can finally sit down and start the long process of writing the book. Each book that Konigsburg writes takes her an average of a full year to a year and a half to complete. In order to stay on schedule, Konigsburg makes sure that she sets aside a certain amount of time each day to write. It takes a lot of discipline, but Konigsburg works hard to make sure she sticks to a writing schedule, although she admits that she has relaxed a little as she's gotten older:

> I'm at my desk every day when I'm here at home. I get up, get dressed, and go to my office, which is my son's old bedroom. I used to be very rigid about my mornings and not even answer the phone. My kids and my husband used to have a signal to give me if I needed to pick up the phone. But now that my children are gone from home, I do take necessary calls. My friends are all very nice; they know that I don't like to take personal calls in the morning.[4]

Konigsburg understands the value of discipline and how it contributes to her success as a writer. When asked what advice she would give to someone who wants to be a writer, she responded, "I always give one word [of advice], and the word is: finish. The word is finish because I think the difference between being a person of talent and being a writer is the ability to apply the seat of your pants to the seat of your chair and finish. It means you'll sit there and . . . that you'll have the discipline to transform talent into a written story, book, whatever."[5]

Elaine Lobl Konigsburg has followed her own advice very well. Her discipline has enabled her to write twenty books so far, which is a remarkably large number for someone who didn't even decide to become a writer until she had spent several years establishing a career in science first. Considering the scientific way that Konigsburg approaches writing, though, perhaps her years of studying science were not really a separate career after all, but merely background research for her life as a writer. However, as she concluded once in an interview, "All in all, I can tell you that my book people are more fun than molecules."[6]

# Interview with E. L. Konigsburg

**RENEE AMBROSEK:** You've created a lot of very strong juvenile characters in your novels. Which character would you consider your favorite and why?

**E. L. KONIGSBURG:** Currently, I am in love with Margaret Rose Kane, the heroine of my newest book, *The Outcasts of 19 Schuyler Place*. The reason? Probably because I first met her as an adult in *Silent to the Bone* and know what a wonderful woman she turned out to be.

**RENEE AMBROSEK:** You've said in interviews that your favorite children's authors are Louisa May Alcott and Frances Hodgkins Burnett, both of whom are classic authors of children's fiction from earlier eras. Do you ever read much contemporary children's literature, and if so, whom would you say are your favorite contemporary children's book authors?

**E. L. KONIGSBURG:** Judy Blume and Judith Viorst.

**RENEE AMBROSEK:** It seems that in many of your books, the main characters are led to a better understanding of themselves through the guidance of an older female character, such as Mrs. Frankweiler, Tallulah, Edie, Caroline, etc. Why are your mentoring characters so often female?

**E. L. KONIGSBURG:** Aside from my late husband, David, women—very often contemporaries—have been my mentors.

**RENEE AMBROSEK:** One of your books was turned into a studio film (*From the Mixed-up Files of Mrs. Basil E. Frankweiler*), and at least three have been made into television movies (*From the Mixed-up Files. . ., Jennifer, Hecate, Macbeth, William McKinley, and Me, Elizabeth,* and *Father's Arcane Daughter*). What do you think of the film adaptations of your work? Is there a work of yours that you would like to see made into a film that hasn't yet been?

**E. L. KONIGSBURG:** Here's the scorecard:

*Jennifer, Hecate, Macbeth, William McKinley, and Me, Elizabeth*: Very long ago, and as abbreviated in my memory as was the production.

*From the Mixed-up Files of Mrs. Basil E. Frankweiler* (studio film with Ingrid Bergman): 8 out of 10.

*Father's Arcane Daughter* (Hallmark Hall of Fame production called Caroline?): 9 out of 10.

*From the Mixed-up Files of Mrs. Basil E. Frankweiler* (ABC special starring Lauren Bacall): something between awful and godawful.

**RENEE AMBROSEK:** Very often your characters have very strong, loving bonds with their siblings, in spite of any sibling rivalry or teasing. What was your relationship with your own two sisters like as you grew up?

**E. L. KONIGSBURG:** Very strong, loving bonds in spite of sibling rivalry or teasing.

**RENEE AMBROSEK:** You've illustrated several of your own books, but not all of them. Why did you choose to add illustrations to some of your books, but not others?

**E. L. KONIGSBURG:** I do not think that illustrations are always necessary to enlarge the story. I have enjoyed doing the art for the jackets of my books, and I have loved doing my three picture books.

**RENEE AMBROSEK:** Which do you enjoy more, writing short stories or novels?

**E. L. KONIGSBURG:** Both the same.

**RENEE AMBROSEK:** You've said that the difference between being just a person with talent and being a writer is that a writer has the discipline to sit in his or her chair and actually finish writing. Is the writing process hard for you? Do you find it difficult to discipline yourself to write?

**E. L. KONIGSBURG:** The distractions now are different in kind but not in degree from when I was a young mother and started writing. So, yes, the discipline required is different but to no degree easier.

**RENEE AMBROSEK:** Many of your characters are outsiders in some way. Why do you so often create characters who are outside of the "norm"?

**E. L. KONIGSBURG:** Outsiders always have a fresh perspective.

**RENEE AMBROSEK:** Your characters all seem to share a very keen sense of humor, and your books and stories are littered with great zingers and one-liners. Do you have a favorite line or funny situation from your books?

**E. L. KONIGSBURG:** Currently, my favorite line is from *The View from Saturday*. Nadia says, "Inside me, there was a lot of best friendship that no one but Ginger was using." [Ginger is Nadia's dog.]

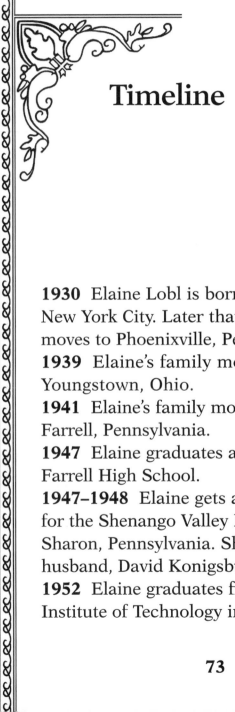

# Timeline

**1930**  Elaine Lobl is born on February 10 in New York City. Later that year, her family moves to Phoenixville, Pennsylvania.

**1939**  Elaine's family moves to Youngstown, Ohio.

**1941**  Elaine's family moves again, this time to Farrell, Pennsylvania.

**1947**  Elaine graduates as valedictorian from Farrell High School.

**1947–1948**  Elaine gets a job keeping books for the Shenango Valley Provision Company in Sharon, Pennsylvania. She meets her future husband, David Konigsburg, at this job.

**1952**  Elaine graduates from Carnegie Mellon Institute of Technology in Pittsburgh with a

BS in chemistry. In July, she marries David Konigsburg.

**1952–1954** Elaine does graduate work in chemistry at the University of Pittsburgh.

**1954** Elaine and David move to Jacksonville, Florida, as a result of David's job.

**1954–1955** Elaine teaches science at the Bartram School in Jacksonville.

**1955** Elaine leaves teaching when her first son, Paul, is born.

**1956** Elaine's daughter, Laurie, is born.

**1959** Elaine's second son, Ross, is born. Elaine begins taking formal painting lessons, and one of her paintings wins first prize in a county fair art competition.

**1960–1962** Elaine returns to teaching science at the Bartram School.

**1962–1963** The Konigsburg family moves to Saddle Brook, New Jersey, and Elaine joins the Art Students League in New York City.

**1963** The Konigsburg family moves again, this time to Port Chester, New York.

**1965** Konigsburg begins writing and illustrating her first book, *Jennifer, Hecate, Macbeth, William McKinley, and Me, Elizabeth.*

**1966** Konigsburg submits her first book to Atheneum Press and begins work on her second book, *From the Mixed-up Files of Mrs. Basil E. Frankweiler.*

**1967** The Konigsburg family moves back to Jacksonville, Florida. Both of Konigsburg's first two books are published in this same year.

**1968** *Files* wins the Newbery Medal, and *Jennifer* wins a Newbery Honor Book award, the only time in history that the same author has had two books on the Newbery list at the same time.

**1969** *About the B'nai Bagels* is published.

**1970** *(George)* is published. *Files* wins the William Allen White Children's Book Award.

**1971** *Altogether, One at a Time* is published. Elaine receives the Carnegie-Mellon Merit Award.

**1973** *A Proud Taste for Scarlet and Miniver* is published. *Files* is made into a film called *The Hideaways*.

**1974** *The Dragon in the Ghetto Caper* is published. *Proud Taste* is named an American Library Association (ALA) Notable Children's Book.

**1975** *The Second Mrs. Giaconda* is published, and it receives the American Library Association's (ALA) Best Book for Young Adults Award.

**1976** *Father's Arcane Daughter* is published, and it also receives the American Library Association's (ALA) Best Book for Young Adults Award. *The*

*Second Mrs. Giaconda* is adapted into a play and is performed in Jacksonville.

**1977** *Daughter* is named an American Library Association (ALA) Notable Book for Young Adults.

**1979** *Throwing Shadows* is published.

**1980** *Throwing Shadows* is named an American Library Association (ALA) Notable Children's Book.

**1982** *Journey to an 800 Number* is published.

**1986** *Up from Jericho Tel* is published.

**1987** *Jericho Tel* is named an American Library Association (ALA) Notable Children's Book.

**1990** The Hallmark Hall of Fame TV movie *Caroline?*, an adaptation of *Father's Arcane Daughter*, premieres. Konigsburg's first picture book for younger children, *Samuel Todd's Book of Great Colors*, is published.

**1991** *Samuel Todd's Book of Great Inventions*, Konigsburg's second picture book, is published.

**1992** *Amy Elizabeth Explores Bloomingdale's*, a third picture book, is published.

**1993** *T-Backs, T-Shirts, COAT and Suit* is published.

**1995** *TalkTalk: A Children's Book Author Speaks to Grown-Ups*, a book of essays for adults, is published.

**1996** *The View from Saturday* is published.

**1997** Konigsburg wins her second Newbery Medal for *The View from Saturday*.

**1999** Konigsburg is given the Distinguished Alumni Achievement Award from Carnegie Mellon University.

**2000** *Silent to the Bone* is published.

**2004** *The Outcasts of 19 Schuyler Place* is published.

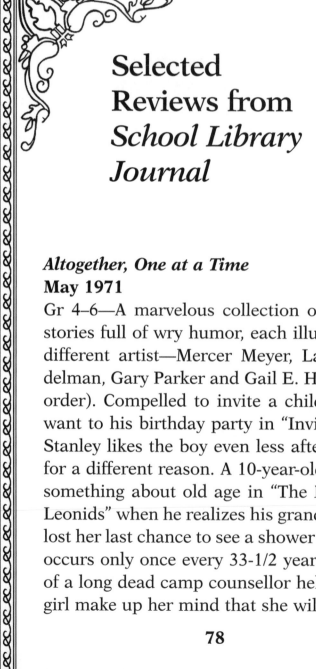

## Selected Reviews from *School Library Journal*

***Altogether, One at a Time***
**May 1971**

Gr 4–6—A marvelous collection of four short stories full of wry humor, each illustrated by a different artist—Mercer Meyer, Laurel Schindelman, Gary Parker and Gail E. Haley (in that order). Compelled to invite a child he doesn't want to his birthday party in "Inviting Jason," Stanley likes the boy even less afterwards, but for a different reason. A 10-year-old boy learns something about old age in "The Night of the Leonids" when he realizes his grandmother has lost her last chance to see a shower of stars that occurs only once every 33-1/2 years. The spirit of a long dead camp counsellor helps an obese girl make up her mind that she will never have to attend Camp Fat again. In "Momma at the Pearly Gates," Momma tells the story of how, as a girl, she was called a "dirty nigger" by a white classmate. Her superb aplomb in handling the situation is both credible and memorable. The author shows the same empathetic insight into the minds and emotions of children that she has displayed in her previous titles.

## From the Mixed-up Files of Mrs. Basil E. Frankweiler
## October 1967

[This] is the kind of book our increasingly sophisticated pre-teens ask for, and it has almost all they hope for in a book: humor, suspense, intrigue, and their problems acknowledged seriously but not somberly. The author has followed her outstanding *Jennifer, Hecate, Macbeth, William McKinley, and Me, Elizabeth* with another excellent book. Claudia, eldest of four children, feels put upon and seeks to escape the tedium of suburban life. Her decision to run away is planned as carefully as a safari; brother Jamie is invited because of his hoard of money. Their destination is the Metropolitan Museum of Art where they elude the security guards and live comfortably for six days. Claudia refuses to consider going home until she's established an admirable identity of her own, one she feels will be acknowledged when she determines the origin of a small statue attributed to Michelangelo. The children's circuitous detecting leads them to the tart, enigmatic Mrs. Frankweiler, last owner of the statue. She helps them return home by making Claudia understand that true individuality is interior—and often secret at that. Anybody rejecting this book on the grounds that resolute Claudia and canny Jamie should not be shown cleverly flouting museum rules or so apparently unconcerned over their parents' anguish would be denying their patrons the reading pleasure of an unusual book, extremely well-written.

### The Outcasts of 19 Schuyler Place
### January 2004

Gr 6–9—In *Silent to the Bone* (Atheneum, 2000), a grown-up Margaret Rose Kane helps her half brother, Connor, solve the mystery of why his best friend can't speak. *Outcasts* is her remembrance of her 12th summer. Pitched into camp by her parents while they travel in Peru, she is tormented by cliquish cabin mates and adopts a passive-aggressive stance that infuriates the overly rigid and money-grasping camp director. Rescued by her beloved elderly uncles and taken to their home, Margaret is appalled to discover that the city has ordered the soaring, artistic towers they have created in the backyard to be taken down because they don't adhere to the strictures of the now-historic district. Stung by the idea that real history and a work of art could be destroyed by profit-seeking interest groups manipulating governmental regulations, Margaret swings into action to fight an even larger tyranny than the one she had encountered at camp. Delicious irony permeates the story, with Margaret citing words from idealistic documents and then relating the reality. The plot is well paced and has excellent foreshadowing. Konigsburg's characters are particularly well motivated, from the camp director who gives herself airs to hide well-earned insecurities, to her seemingly mentally challenged son who is actually an intellectual as well as an artist. Most wonderfully rendered through dialogue are the Hungarian-American Jewish uncles, crotchety with age, but full of love and life and a sure understanding of what it means to be an individual American. Funny and thought-provoking by turns, this is Konigsburg at her masterful best.

### *The Second Mrs. Giaconda*
### September 1975

Gr 7 Up—The riddle of the Mona Lisa is solved in a most ingenious reconstruction of the middle years of Leonardo da Vinci's life. Under Konigsburg's deft hand the bare bones of history are fleshed out with some remarkable characters, especially the street urchin, Salai, who becomes servant and companion to Leonardo, and the Duchess Beatrice of Milan, the young wife of Leonardo's patron. The interaction of these personalities and their influence on the master are the focus of the novel and finally explain why, in later years, Leonardo refused great commissions to paint Duchesses and great ladies, and chose, instead, to grant immortality to an unknown merchant's wife, the Second Mrs. Giaconda. Based on the known facts of Leonardo's life and times, Konigsburg uses this information not just as a framework for the retelling of history, but as a living clay from which a thoroughly entertaining and believable story is molded. The result is a unique bit of creative historical interpretation, and a slice of Renaissance life artfully and authentically illuminated.

### *Silent to the Bone*
### September 2000

Gr 6–8—Branwell Zamborska, 13, is struck dumb on the day that his baby half sister slips into a coma. From the novel's opening, a tape of the 911 call from the Zamborska's residence to the emergency operator, readers are immediately engaged in the story. Did Branwell drop the baby, as the family's

British au pair claims? Nikki is taken to the hospital; Branwell to a juvenile behavioral center. Bran's best friend, Connor Kane, devises a way to communicate with the mute boy through flashcards and, with the help of his older half sister, Margaret, is able to find out what actually happened to Nikki. It is shame that has caused Branwell to shut down. His adolescent sexuality has been awakened by the au pair, who bathes in front of him and spends afternoons in her bedroom with the pizza delivery man. Bran's body's response to seeing her breasts makes him feel ashamed and unable to tell his parents that Vivian is mistreating the baby. From not speaking, he goes to being unable to speak. Connor is able to help Branwell speak the truth, Nikki recovers, and the blended Zamborska family is reunited in a touching final scene where Bran's genuine love of his little sister is evident and accepted by his stepmother. Part detective and suspense story, this multilayered novel is much more, touching on themes of communication, relationships in blended families, being different, friendship, adolescence, and shame. In a wonderful joining of characterization and narrative style, Connor's voice shines throughout the novel. It is cleverly written, and full of wit, plot twists, and engaging characters.

*The View from Saturday*
**September 1996**

Gr 4–6—Take four sixth graders; combine them as the Epiphany School team for Academic Bowl; add one paraplegic teacher; toss in formal tea times, grandparents of team members getting married, and some magic and calligraphy. Stir them with Konigsburg's masterful hand and you have an ingenious story. Nadia, Noah, Julian, and Ethan are not the top honor students, but Mrs. Olinski has chosen them for other reasons, ones unclear even to her. As the team beats all odds and expectations and reaches the finals, flashbacks told by each member shape a scenario that's like a bundle of pick-up sticks, each piece touching, supporting, and overlapping with the others, and one move effects them all. Stunning interplay of Nadia's turtle watches on Florida beaches, Noah's role as best man at a senior-citizen wedding, Ethan's discovery of himself through new friends, and Julian's ethical decision involving a bully skillfully wrap their stories into one, with amazing insights. Brilliant writing melds with crystalline characterizations in this sparkling story that is a jewel in the author's crown of out-standing work.

Selected reviews from *School Library Journal* reproduced with permission from *School Library Journal*, copyright © 1967, 1971, 1975, 1996, 2000, 2004 by Cahners Business Information, a division of Reed Elsevier, Inc.

# List of
# Selected Works

*About the B'nai Bagels*. New York, NY: Atheneum, 1969.

*Altogether, One at a Time*. New York, NY: Atheneum, 1971.

*Amy Elizabeth Explores Bloomingdale's*. New York, NY: Atheneum, 1992.

*The Dragon in the Ghetto Caper*. New York, NY: Atheneum, 1974.

*Father's Arcane Daughter*. New York, NY: Atheneum, 1976.

*From the Mixed-up Files of Mrs. Basil E. Frankweiler*. New York, NY: Aladdin Paperbacks, 2002.

*(George)*. New York, NY: Atheneum, 1970.

*Jennifer, Hecate, Macbeth, William McKinley, and Me, Elizabeth*. New York, NY: Atheneum, 1967.

*Journey to an 800 Number*. New York, NY: Atheneum, 1982.

*The Outcasts of 19 Schuyler Place*. New York, NY: Atheneum, 2004.

*A Proud Taste for Scarlet and Miniver*. New York, NY: Atheneum, 1973.

*Samuel Todd's Book of Great Colors*. New York, NY: Macmillan, 1990.

*Samuel Todd's Book of Great Inventions*. New York, NY: Atheneum, 1991.

*The Second Mrs. Giaconda*. New York, NY: Atheneum, 1975.

*Silent to the Bone*. New York, NY: Atheneum, 2000.

*TalkTalk: A Children's Book Author Speaks to Grown-Ups*. New York, NY: Atheneum, 1995.

*T-Backs, T-Shirts, COAT and Suit*. New York, NY: Atheneum, 1993.

*Throwing Shadows*. New York, NY: Atheneum, 1979.

*Up from Jericho Tel*. New York, NY: Atheneum, 1986.

*The View from Saturday*. New York, NY: Atheneum, 1996.

# List of
# Selected Awards

Carnegie-Mellon Merit Award (1971)
Distinguished Alumni Achievement Award—
　Carnegie Mellon University (1999)
Special Recognition Award from the Cultural
　Council of Greater Jacksonville (1997)

***About the B'nai Bagels*** **(1969)**
The Child Study Association of America's
　Children's Book of the Year (1969)

***Father's Arcane Daughter*** **(1976)**
American Library Association (ALA) Best Book
　for Young Adults Selection (1977)

***From the Mixed-up Files of Mrs. Basil E.***
***Frankweiler*** **(1967)**

Lewis Carroll Shelf Award (1968)
Newbery Medal (1968)
William Allen White Award (1970)

### *Jennifer, Hecate, Macbeth, William McKinley, and Me, Elizabeth* (1967)
Book Week Spring Book Festival Honor
Book (1967)
The Child Study Association of America's Children's
Book of the Year (1967)
Newbery Honor Book (1968)

### *Journey to an 800 Number* (1982)
The Child Study Association of America's Children's
Book of the Year (1982)

### *A Proud Taste for Scarlet and Miniver* (1973)
American Library Association (ALA) Notable
Children's Book (1974)
The Child Study Association of America's Children's
Book of the Year (1973)
National Book Nomination (1974)

### *The Second Mrs. Giaconda* (1975)
American Library Association (ALA) Best Book
for Young Adults Selection (1975)

### *Throwing Shadows* (1979)

American Book Award Nomination (1980)

American Library Association (ALA) Notable
Children's Book (1980)

### *Up from Jericho Tel* (1986)

American Library Association (ALA) Notable
Children's Book (1987)

Notable Children's Trade Book for the Language
Arts, from the National Council of the Teachers
of English (1987)

Parent's Choice Award for Literature (1987)

### *The View from Saturday* (1996)

Newbery Medal (1997)

# Glossary

**acetone** A flammable, organic liquid compound that is often used as a solvent in products ranging from pharmaceuticals to paint.

**avid** Desirous or eager.

**Bunsen burner** A gas burner, used in laboratories, with an air valve that regulates the mixture of gas and air. This mixture produces an intense blue flame.

**concentric** To have a common center or axis.

**genre** A category of art, music, or literature that shares characteristics particular to that form.

**Great Depression** A period of about ten years of worldwide economic crisis, beginning with the stock market crash on October 28, 1929.

During this time, many businesses collapsed and many families were poverty-stricken.

**May I?**  A childhood game, also known as "Mother, May I?" One child acts as "Mom" and faces away from the line of other children. "Mom" then chooses a child and gives him or her a direction. The child must respond with "Mother, May I?" If the child forgets this response, he or she must go back to the beginning of the line. The first to touch "Mom" wins.

**Newbery Medal**  An award given every year to the most distinguished contribution to American children's literature. The Newbery Committee also gives a number of Newbery Honor awards each year to books considered to be of special merit.

**Pick-up Sticks**  A childhood game in which the player holds multicolored sticks upright and altogether in one hand, then drops the sticks and lets them scatter. The object of the game is to pick up as many sticks as possible, without making another stick move. Black sticks are worth more points.

***The Secret Garden***  A children's novel by Francis Hodgson Burnett, first published in 1911. In this classic story, the orphaned young girl, Mary Lennox, goes to live at her uncle's great house. She soon learns it is full of secrets. Mary befriends a boy who can talk to the animals and discovers a secret garden that has been forgotten for many years.

**Statue**  A game where one player is the shop-keeper, another player is the buyer, and the rest are statues. After being spun around and let go by the shopkeeper, the "statues" remain in the position they fell in and think up a statue for that position. The buyer then comes in and watches each statue demonstrate what they are supposed to be, before deciding which one to buy.

**veneer**  A superficial or deceptive appearance.

**war bond**  At the time of World War II, this was an "I owe you" contract between the government (the issuer) and the bond holder (the buyer). In order to raise money for the war effort, the government appealed to Americans to buy bonds as a show of patriotism. The government paid the buyer the interest on the debt while it was outstanding and then redeemed the bond by paying back the debt.

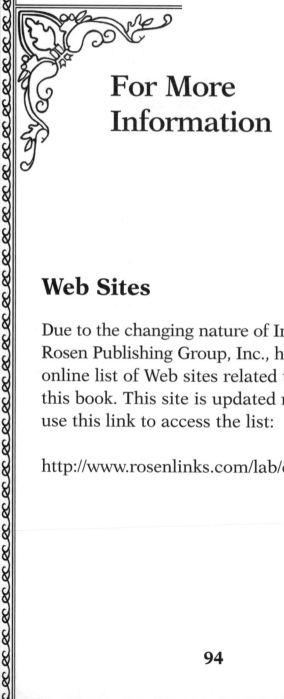

# For More Information

## Web Sites

Due to the changing nature of Internet links, the Rosen Publishing Group, Inc., has developed an online list of Web sites related to the subject of this book. This site is updated regularly. Please use this link to access the list:

http://www.rosenlinks.com/lab/elko

# For Further Reading

Commire, Anne. *Something About the Author*, Vol. 4. Detroit, MI: Gale Research, 1973.

Hoffman, Miriam, and Eva Samuels, eds. *Authors and Illustrators of Children's Books: Writing on Their Lives and Works*. New York, NY: Bowker, 1972.

Kingman, Lee, ed. *Newbery and Caldecott Medal Books 1966–1975*. Boston, MA: Horn Book, Inc., 1975.

Konigsburg, E. L. *TalkTalk: A Children's Book Author Speaks to Grown-Ups*. New York, NY: Atheneum, 1995.

Marcus, Leonard S., ed. *Author Talk*. New York, NY: Simon & Schuster Books for Young Readers, 2000.

Salvadore, Maria, Roger Sutton, and Kathleen Horning. *The Newbery and Caldecott Medal Books 1986–2000: A Comprehensive Guide to the Winners*. Boston, MA: American Library Association, 2001.

Townsend, John Rowe. *A Sounding of Storytellers*. New York, NY: Lippincot, Williams & Wilkins, 1979.

# Bibliography

Bregman, Alice Miller. Review of *A Proud Taste for Scarlet and Miniver*. *School Library Journal*, October 1973, p. 117.

Commire, Anne. "E. L. Konigsburg." *Something About the Author*, Vol. 4. Detroit, MI: Gale Research, 1973.

Cummins, Julie. Review of *The View from Saturday*. *School Library Journal*, September 1996, p. 204.

"E. L. Konigsburg's Interview Transcript." Scholastic.com. Retrieved November 10, 2004 (http://www2.scholastic.com/teachers/authorsandbooks/authorstudies/authorhome.jhtml?authorID=644&collateralID=5342&displayName=Interview+Transcript&displayName=Interview%20Transcript).

"EPA's Top 100 Authors: E. L. Konigsburg." Educational Paperback Association. Retrieved September 1, 2004 (http://www.edupaperback.org/showauth.cfm?authid=169).

Gibson, Campbell J., and Emily Lennon. "Historical Census Statistics on the Foreign-born Population of the United States: 1850–1990." U.S. Census Bureau. Retrieved September 1, 2004 (http://www.census.gov/population/www/documentation/twps0029/twps0029.html).

Hanks, Dorrel Thomas, Jr. *E. L. Konigsburg*. New York, NY: Twayne Publishers, 1992.

Heins, Paul. Review of *A Proud Taste for Scarlet and Miniver*. *Horn Book Magazine*, October 1973, p. 466.

Hoffman, Miriam, and Eva Samuels, eds. *Authors and Illustrators of Children's Books: Writing on Their Lives and Works*. New York, NY: Bowker, 1972.

Jones, Daniel, and John Jorgenson, eds. "E. L. Konigsburg." *Contemporary Authors New Revision*, Vol. 59. Detroit, MI: Gale Research, 1998.

Jones, Linda T. "Profile: Elaine Konigsburg." *Language Arts*, February 1986, pp. 177–184.

Karl, Jean. "Elaine L. Konigsburg," *School Library Journal*, March 1968, pp. 111–112.

Kingman, Lee, ed. *Newbery and Caldecott Medal Books 1966–1975*. Boston, MA: Horn Book, Inc., 1975.

Konigsburg, David. "Elaine Konigsburg." *Newbery and Caldecott Medal Books 1966–1975*. Boston, MA: Horn Book, Inc., 1975.

Konigsburg, Elaine Lobl. "A Book Is a Private Thing." *Saturday Review*, November 9, 1968, pp. 45–46.

Konigsburg, E. L. *About the B'nai Bagels*. New York, NY: Atheneum, 1969.

Konigsburg, E. L. *Altogether, One at a Time*. New York, NY: Atheneum, 1971.

Konigsburg, E. L. *Amy Elizabeth Explores Bloomingdale's*. New York, NY: Atheneum, 1992.

Konigsburg, E. L. *The Dragon in the Ghetto Caper*. New York, NY: Atheneum, 1974.

Konigsburg, E. L. *Father's Arcane Daughter*. New York, NY: Atheneum, 1976.

Konigsburg, E. L. *Forty Percent More Than Everything You Want to Know About E. L. Konigsburg*. New York, NY: Atheneum, 1974.

Konigsburg, E. L. *From the Mixed-up Files of Mrs. Basil E. Frankweiler*. New York, NY: Atheneum, 1967.

Konigsburg, E. L. *(George)*. New York, NY: Atheneum, 1970.

Konigsburg, E. L. *Jennifer, Hecate, Macbeth, William McKinley, and Me, Elizabeth*. New York, NY: Atheneum, 1967.

Konigsburg, E. L. *Journey to an 800 Number*. New York, NY: Atheneum, 1982.

Konigsburg, E. L. "Newbery Award Acceptance Speech." *Newbery and Caldecott Medal Books 1966–1975*. Boston, MA: Horn Book, Inc., 1975.

Konigsburg, E. L. *The Outcasts of 19 Schuyler Place*. New York, NY: Atheneum, 2004.

Konigsburg, E. L. *A Proud Taste for Scarlet and Miniver*. New York, NY: Atheneum, 1973.

Konigsburg, E. L. *Samuel Todd's Book of Great Colors*. New York, NY: Macmillan, 1990.

Konigsburg, E. L. *Samuel Todd's Book of Great Inventions*. New York, NY: Atheneum, 1991.

Konigsburg, E. L. *The Second Mrs. Giaconda*. New York, NY: Atheneum, 1975.

Konigsburg, E. L. *Silent to the Bone*. New York, NY: Atheneum, 2000.

Konigsburg, E. L. *TalkTalk: A Children's Book Author Speaks to Grown-Ups*. New York, NY: Atheneum, 1995.

Konigsburg, E. L. *T-Backs, T-Shirts, COAT and Suit*. New York, NY: Atheneum, 1993.

Konigsburg, E. L. *Throwing Shadows*. New York, NY: Atheneum, 1979.

Konigsburg, E. L. *Up from Jericho Tel*. New York, NY: Atheneum, 1986.

Konigsburg, E. L. *The View from Saturday*. New York, NY: Atheneum, 1996.

Marcus, Leonard S., ed. *Author Talk*. New York, NY: Simon & Schuster Books for Young Readers, 2000.

Metzger, Linda, and Deborah A. Straub, eds. *Contemporary Authors New Revision*, Vol. 17. Detroit, MI: Gale Research, 1986.

*The Newbery and Caldecott Medal Books 1986–2000: A Comprehensive Guide to the Winners*. Boston, MA: Horn Book and American Library Association, 2001.

Nodelman, Perry. "E. L. Konigsburg." *Dictionary of Literary Biography, Vol. 52: American Writers for Children Since 1960—Fiction*. Detroit, MI: Gale Research, 1986, pp. 214–227.

Peacock, Scot, ed. *Contemporary Authors New Revision*, Vol. 106. Detroit, MI: Gale Research, 2002.

Rees, David. "Your Arcane Novelist—E. L. Konigsburg." *Horn Book Magazine*, February 1978, pp. 79–85.

Roback, Diane, and Jason Britton, eds. "All-Time Bestselling Children's Books." PublishersWeekly.com. Retrieved September 1,

2004 (http://www.publishersweekly.com/article/CA186995.html?pubdate=12%2F17%2F2001&display=archive).

Todd, Laurie Konigsburg. "E. L. Konigsburg." *The Newbery and Caldecott Medal Books 1986–2000*. Chicago, IL: The Horn Book Association for Library Service to Children, 2001.

Trosky, Susan M., ed. *Contemporary Authors New Revision*, Vol. 39. Detroit, MI: Gale Research, 1992, pp. 207–211.

Winchester, Elizabeth. "Meet E. L. Konigsburg." Time for Kids Online. Retrieved September 1, 2004 (http://www.timeforkids.com/TFK/news/story/0,6260,601429,00.html).

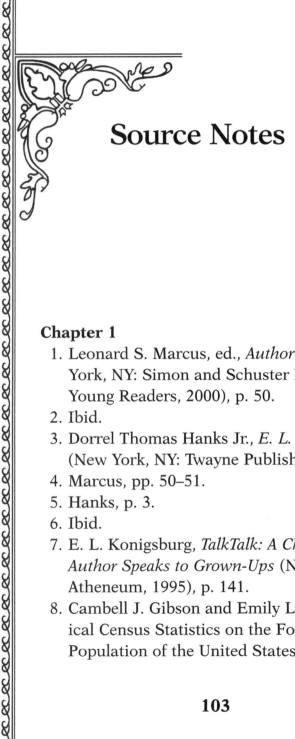

# Source Notes

**Chapter 1**

1. Leonard S. Marcus, ed., *Author Talk* (New York, NY: Simon and Schuster Books for Young Readers, 2000), p. 50.
2. Ibid.
3. Dorrel Thomas Hanks Jr., *E. L. Konigsburg* (New York, NY: Twayne Publishers, 1992) p. 2.
4. Marcus, pp. 50–51.
5. Hanks, p. 3.
6. Ibid.
7. E. L. Konigsburg, *TalkTalk: A Children's Book Author Speaks to Grown-Ups* (New York, NY: Atheneum, 1995), p. 141.
8. Cambell J. Gibson and Emily Lennon, "Historical Census Statistics on the Foreign-born Population of the United States: 1850–1990."

U.S. Census Bureau. Retrieved September 1, 2004 (http://www.census.gov/population/www/documentation/twps0029/twps0029.html).

9. Marcus, p. 51.
10. Konigsburg, p. 15.
11. Linda T. Jones, "Profile: Elaine Kongisburg," *Language Arts*, February 1986, p. 178.
12. Konigsburg, p. 140.

**Chapter 2**

1. Daniel Jones and John Jorgenson, eds., "E. L. Konigsburg," *Contemporary Authors New Revision Series*, Vol. 59 (Detroit, MI: Gale Research, 1998), p. 221.
2. "E. L. Konigsburg," in Linda Metzger and Deborah A. Straub, eds., *Contemporary Authors New Revision Series*, Vol. 17 (Detroit, MI: Gale Research, 1986), p. 251.
3. Dorrel Thomas Hanks Jr., *E. L. Konigsburg* (New York, NY: Twayne Publishers, 1992), p. 4.
4. Leonard S. Marcus, ed., *Author Talk* (New York, NY: Simon and Schuster Books for Young Readers, 2000), p. 51.
5. "E. L. Konigsburg," in Susan M. Trosky, ed., *Contemporary Authors New Revision Series*, Vol. 39 (Detroit, MI: Gale Research, 1992), p. 208.
6. Jean Karl, "Elaine L. Konigsburg," *School Library Journal*, March 1968, p. 112.
7. Marcus, p. 52.

8. Jones and Jorgenson, p. 222.
9. Ibid.
10. Hanks, p. 6.
11. Jones and Jorgenson, p. 222.
12. Ibid.

## Chapter 3

1. E. L. Konigsburg, *TalkTalk: A Children's Book Author Speaks to Grown-Ups* (New York, NY: Atheneum, 1995), p. 71.
2. Ibid., p. 73.
3. Anne Commire, "E. L. Konigsburg," *Something About the Author*, Vol. 4 (Detroit, MI: Gale Research, 1973), p. 138.
4. Konigsburg, p. 19.
5. Jean Karl, "Elaine L. Konigsburg," *School Library Journal*, March 1968, p. 111.
6. Ibid.
7. E. L. Konigsburg, *Forty Percent More Than Everything You Want to Know About E. L. Konigsburg* (New York, NY: Atheneum, 1995).
8. E. L. Konigsburg, *From the Mixed-up Files of Mrs. Basil E. Frankweiler* (New York, NY: Aladdin Paperbacks, 2002), p. 14–15.
9. Karl, pp. 111–112.

## Chapter 4

1. Jean Karl, "Elaine L. Konigsburg," *School Library Journal*, March 1968, p. 112.

2. David Konigsburg, "Elaine Konigsburg," *Newbery and Caldecott Medal Books 1966–1975* (Boston, MA: Horn Book, Inc., 1975), p. 44.

3. E. L. Konigsburg, *About the B'nai Bagels* (New York, NY: Atheneum, 1969), p. 6.

4. Linda T. Jones, "Profile: Elaine Konigsburg," *Language Arts*, February 1986, pp. 178–179.

5. Leonard S. Marcus, ed., *Author Talk* (New York, NY: Simon and Schuster Books for Young Readers, 2000), p. 52.

6. Laurie Konigsburg Todd, "E. L. Konigsburg," *The Newbery and Caldecott Medal Books 1986–2000*, (Chicago, IL: The Horn Book Association for Library Service to Children, 2001), p. 276.

7. Diane Roback and Jason Britton, eds., "All-Time Bestselling Children's Books." PublishersWeekly.com. Retrieved September 1, 2004 (http://www.publishersweekly.com/article/ CA186995.html?pubdate=12%2F17%2F2001& display=archive).

8. "E. L. Konigsburg," in Linda Metzger and Deborah A. Straub, eds., *Contemporary Authors New Revision Series*, Vol. 17 (Detroit, MI: Gale Research, 1986), p. 253.

9. "EPA's Top 100 Authors: E. L. Konigsburg." Educational Paperback Association. Retrieved September 1, 2004 (http://www.edupaperback.org/ showauth.cfm?authid=169).

## Chapter 5

1. "E. L. Konigsburg," in Linda Metzger and Deborah A. Straub, eds., *Contemporary Authors New Revision Series*, Vol. 17 (Detroit, MI: Gale Research, 1986), p. 253.
2. David Rees, "Your Arcane Novelist—E. L. Konigsburg," *Horn Book Magazine*, February 1978, p. 81.
3. Linda T. Jones, "Profile: Elaine Konigsburg," *Language Arts*, February 1986, pp. 179–180.
4. Alice Miller Bregman, Review of *A Proud Taste for Scarlet and Miniver*, *School Library Journal*, October 1973, p. 117.
5. Paul Heins, Review of *A Proud Taste for Scarlet and Miniver*, *Horn Book Magazine*, October 1973, p. 466.
6. Perry Nodelman, "E. L. Konigsburg," *Dictionary of Literary Biography, Vol. 52: American Writers for Children Since 1960—Fiction* (Detroit, MI: Gale Research, 1986), p. 224.
7. Julie Cummins, Review of *The View from Saturday*, *School Library Journal*, September 1996, p. 204.
8. Laurie Konigsburg Todd, "E. L. Konigsburg," *The Newbery and Caldecott Medal Books 1986-2000*, (Chicago, IL: The Horn Book Association for Library Service to Children, 2001), p. 276.
9. Elizabeth Winchester, "Meet E. L. Konigsburg," Time for Kids Online. Retrieved September 1, 2004

(http://www.timeforkids.com/TFK/news/story/
0,6260,601429,00.html).

**Chapter 6**

1. "E. L. Konigsburg Interview Transcript."
   Scholastic.com. Retrieved November 10, 2004
   (http://www2.scholastic.com/teachers/
   authorsandbooks/authorstudies/authorhome.jhtml?
   authorID=644&collateralID=5342&displayName=
   Interview+Transcript&displayName=Interview%
   20Transcript).
2. Linda T. Jones, "Profile: Elaine Konigsburg,"
   *Language Arts*, February 1986, p. 182.
3. Jean Karl, "Elaine L. Konigsburg," *School Library
   Journal*, March 1968, p. 112.
4. "E. L. Konigsburg," in Linda Metzger and Deborah
   A. Straub, eds., *Contemporary Authors New
   Revision Series*, Vol. 17 (Detroit, MI: Gale Research,
   1986), p. 252.
5. "E. L. Konigsburg Interview Transcript."
6. Anne Commire, "E. L. Konigsburg," *Something
   About the Author*, Vol. 4 (Detroit, MI: Gale
   Research, 1973), p. 137.

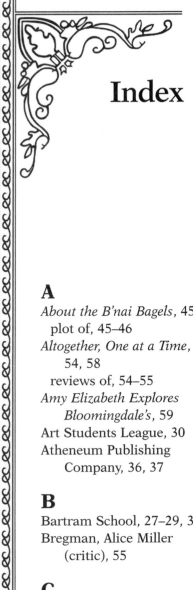

# Index

**110**

# About the Author

Renee Ambrosek is a writer living in Memphis, Tennessee. She has published two nonfiction books for young readers under her married name, Renee Graves. She is currently working on developing a series of historical fiction for young adults. While researching this book, Renee found a quote from E. L. Konigsburg, which stated that the difference between a person with talent and a writer was that a writer actually sits in a chair and writes until the book is finished. Renee is attempting to follow Ms. Konigsburg's advice to finish.

# Photo Credits

Cover, p. 2 © Ron Kunzman.

Designer: Tahara Anderson
Editor: Leigh Ann Cobb
Photo Researcher: Hillary Arnold